From *the* Heart
of a Father

From *the* Heart *of a* Father

Godly Counsel *from* Proverbs

JERRY DRACE

Foreword by David Dockery

DOVE INSPIRATIONAL PRESS
GRETNA 2010

Library of Congress Cataloging-in-Publication Data

Drace, Jerry.
  From the heart of a father : godly counsel from Proverbs / by
Jerry Drace ; foreword by David Dockery.
      p. cm.
  ISBN 978-1-58980-749-5 (hardcover : alk. paper)
1. Fathers—Religious life. 2. Fatherhood—Religious
aspects—Christianity. 3. Bible. O.T. Proverbs—Criticism,
interpretation, etc. I. Title.
  BV4529.17.D73 2010
  248.8′421—dc22
                                    2009039513

*Unless otherwise stated, Scripture quotations in this book are from
the Holman Christian Standard Bible.*

Printed in the United States of America

Published by Dove Inspirational Press, an imprint of Pelican
    Publishing Company, Inc.
1000 Burmaster Street, Gretna, Louisiana 70053

To Drew and Becca and every father who truly loves his children as I do mine

In memory of two fathers who exemplified the teachings found in this book, Bruce Stephens and Andy Harrell

Contents

Foreword

The apostle Paul encourages fathers to bring up their children in the training and instruction of the Lord (Eph. 6:4). Certainly, this word from the apostle was a high calling and lofty challenge for first-century fathers, and it remains such for fathers in the twenty-first century as well. Fathers, along with mothers, are to provide the classroom—the environment, the setting—in which children are introduced to the things of God. A goal of child rearing is for fathers to help children come to the place of accepting God's rule in their lives in a real and personal way.

Fathers are called to be spiritual leaders in the home. Godly instruction and spiritual discipline are to be carried out in wise and loving ways. Fathers are responsible for modeling Christlike behavior for their families, while providing for their physical well-being.

Based on the wise teachings and exhortations found in the Book of Proverbs, Jerry Drace has provided insightful guidance to fathers to help them carry out these responsibilities. In the book that you hold in your hands, Drace has reminded his readers that children are gifts from God (Ps. 127:4-5). Readers are encouraged to recognize that children are gifts to return to God. Children need love, significance, and security. By employing a practical commentary on the Book of Proverbs, Drace helps guide his readers to understand the need to provide tender discipline and discerning instruction. Such discipline should never be done in anger or in an arbitrary manner. The goal of discipline and instruction is to establish boundaries and guidelines for children.

Proverbs 22:6 gives us a helpful word. Parents are encouraged to raise up a child in his or her way. Wise fathers and mothers know that children are different and that not all nonconformity is self-styled rebellion. The goal of Christian parenting is to direct children according to their interests and gifts. The goal for fathers then is to help children move toward godly living in whatever God-honoring direction their lives may take.

Edna Ferber's novel *Giant* is an interesting story about a Texas millionaire named Jordan Benedict. Benedict owned a 2.5 million-acre cattle ranch. His wife was miserable, and he was furious because his young son refused to ride horses. In the novel, Benedict said, "I rode horses before I could walk." His wife responded, "That was you. This is another person. Maybe he just doesn't like horses." The Texas millionaire replied, "He's a Benedict and I'm going to make a horseman out of him if I have to tie him to it."

From the Heart of a Father helps us see that as fathers we are not to force our children into a preconceived mold. Our responsibility, at formal times and at informal times, is to instruct them in God's ways so that their lives can be holy and pleasing in God's sight. Jerry Drace has written a commendable volume that will give guidance to fathers, helping them with formal and informal times of instruction, for we recognize that things are often more caught than taught. Drace calls for fathers to provide children with a sound basis for making decisions. Loving, caring guidance all along the way will help children mature in their choices. I pray that God will use this volume to help the next generation of fathers in the high and lofty calling that is theirs.

DAVID S. DOCKERY
President, Union University

Personal Word from Billy Graham

"The best work in the world is a man or woman doing what God has called them to do and doing it faithfully. Jerry Drace is that kind of individual. His ministry is one of integrity, and he has remained faithful to God's call to evangelism."

BILLY GRAHAM

Acknowledgments

Being a father is the third greatest joy in my life. The first is being a Christian, and the second is being a husband. From standing beside the bed in the neonatal unit at General Hospital in Jacksonville, Florida, when our son Drew was born to being in the delivery room at Baptist Hospital in Jacksonville when our daughter Becca entered the world, fatherhood has been an adventure. As an evangelist, I promised my lovely wife, Becky, that I would never take more than twenty-five engagements a year. God has allowed me to keep that promise. I was there for my children's first steps. I was there in Ridgecrest, North Carolina, when Drew, four, and Becca, two, sang in front of two thousand high-school students. I was there when they broke their first boards in their tae kwon do class and a few years later when they received their first-degree black belts. Becky and I were beside them when they took their first bicycle rides and falls. I coached their church basketball teams and sat in the stands when Becca set the school record for the most three-pointers in a season. I watched as Drew received his third-degree black belt and became an instructor. I was there the day Drew drove out of the driveway for the first time after receiving his driver's license. I went through the same prayer-producing experience when Becca disappeared down the hill in her first car. Believe me; I was there when she had her first official date. I was with Drew when he shot his first duck on that cold December day. When our children started college and when they graduated, I was there wondering how all those experiences had gone by so quickly. As I performed Becca and Josh's wedding, I was there wishing somehow she could be a little girl again. When Drew received his first major job and purchased his first townhouse, Becky and I were there admiring the young man he had become. The journey is not over, but come what may I wouldn't trade being a father for anything is this world.

All present-day fathers are in many involuntary ways reflections of our ancestors. We are like ripples on a still lake adding to an ever-widening circle. Our attitudes, viewpoints, opinions, and ideas about parenting began forming when the first father made the first splash.

I wish to express my deep gratitude to Dr. Pam Sutton, professor of English at Union University in Jackson, Tennessee. Her suggestions, comments, and editing skills made my task a great deal easier. I would also like to thank Heather Green, my editor at Pelican. Her grammatical expertise makes reading this book an enjoyable experience. It is one thing to write a book, making it readable is quite another. Thanks Pam and Heather.

Introduction

There once lived a man who had more children than he could count. This man had seven hundred wives and three hundred concubines as recorded in 1 Kings 11:3. A concubine was a wife of inferior rank to the proper wife. She had no share in the government of the family, and her children were not entitled to a portion of their father's inheritance. This man was Solomon. Although he was often called the wisest man who ever lived, knowing his marital status, wise hardly seems the right word to describe this son of King David.

From the time he could crawl around the palace, Solomon observed his father who was a man after God's own heart according to Acts 13:22. His godly mother, Bathsheba, had learned a bitter lesson earlier in life. His private tutor was the wise, God-fearing prophet Nathan. Solomon was born to nobility but failed to live a noble life. He gave godly counsel to his children but failed to obey the counsel of God.

In order to understand the profound wisdom of the proverbs Solomon shared with his children, you need to look deeply into the life of this extraordinary man as written down in the books of Samuel, Chronicles, and Psalms penned by his father. Dads, the godly counsel and advice you share with your children is not original. It has been passed down from generations with revision, refinement, and reassessment. Nevertheless, it comes from your mouth hopefully after having passed through your heart. Solomon's counsel is as fresh and trustworthy today as when his scribes dipped their quills into their inkwells and recorded on papyri what we know as the Book of Proverbs. The Hebrew word *mishlei* translated "proverbs" is derived from the root word *mashal*, which means "to rule." Therefore, proverbs are words and sayings that assist in ruling and governing life. The one striking feature about this book of profound counsel is that Solomon himself did not follow his own rules. If we want our children to listen, then we as fathers must conform to our own counsel and walk what we talk.

In our society, where over 36 percent of the children live absent from their biological father and over nineteen million live with just their mother, we need fathers to be accountable for their actions. In our society, where over one million children experience the trauma of divorce each year and one out of every six is a stepchild, we need husbands who are committed to their wives and children. In our society, where 40 percent of the children who live in fatherless households haven't seen their fathers in a least a year and 50 percent of children who don't live with their fathers have never stepped foot in their father's home, we need dads who are dependable. Biologically, almost any male can father a child, but there is a vast difference between fathering and parenting. As you read the following counsel from Solomon, may the truth of his instructions be passed on to your children from the heart of a father.

1

Key Words

Key words appear throughout Proverbs. Once you understand the meaning and intent behind these words, these sayings of knowledge open like a treasure chest. In chapter 1, verse 2, you find the principle word in Proverbs—*wisdom*. This word means "moral and religious intelligence." Before anything else, Solomon wanted his children to possess a standard of goodness and rightness in both character and conduct. He knew that one could be ethical without necessarily being moral, since ethical implies conformity with a code of fair and honest behavior. A moral person goes out of his way to avoid the appearance of immorality. When religion and morality are combined in an individual, the result is a person worthy of emulating, especially if that person is a father.

The word *instruction* is found after wisdom. This implies "submission to a higher authority" or "to be disciplined." All people are under someone's authority whether they acknowledge it or not. The CEO of a major company maintains that position only if they can produce consistent growth. The president of the United States answers to Congress and the American people. The military can be effective only as long as submission to higher authority is maintained. A father needs to teach his children the value of submission by demonstrating his submission to the teachings of Holy Scripture. Voluntary submission is always the best. This originates in the heart and responds with outward obedience.

The word *understanding* is often translated as "perceive" and means to distinguish between right and wrong. Solomon wanted his children to make the right decisions. Our postmodern culture teaches there are no absolutes. Our children are taught everything is negotiable. What may be right for one may not be right for another. The Bible teaches the difference between right and wrong and the consequences for making the wrong choices. What postmodernism calls opinions the Bible often calls sin. The Holy Scriptures were not given so we could vote on its validity, but that we might obey its truthfulness.

The fourth word in verse 2 is *insightful* or *understanding*. These words are synonymous with intelligence and discernment. This type of understanding comes from the learning we receive in formal education. That is why schooling is vital for children. They need to be able to understand the complexities of the world in which they live. As the saying goes, "A mind is a terrible thing to waste." A discerning spirit often accompanies an alert mind. This gift is priceless in our world of deceit, duplicity, and double-dealing.

Verse 3 has four key words. The first is *receive*. The implication means to acquire at all cost. Any investment in obtaining wisdom is worthy of its price. Only wisdom can explain the complexity of the following three words in this verse.

Righteousness in this context has to do with your way of life. The course of your life obviously determines your final destination. As a father, as captain of your family ship, your sails must always be set to catch the winds that blow from the breath of God. His settings are always the best. His compass is always true. His seas, though rough at times, will always yield the greatest treasures and land you at the safest harbor.

Justice is to be understood as that of right conduct. If we as fathers are men of right conduct, then chances are our children will be the same. We are told in Psalm 1:1, "How happy is the man who does not follow the advice of the wicked, or take the path of sinners, or join a group of mockers." In other words, our conduct is to be above reproach.

Integrity is the fourth word and closes this verse. Being on the level, being honest is the significance of this word. Your life speaks for itself without resorting to words. Your children watch you 24/7 when they are young and when they are old. Their eyes never close. You never stop being a father.

Verse 4 continues with the reasons for obtaining wisdom. The word *shrewdness* means insight, to know why you do what you do. Sometimes when you ask a child, or even a teenager, why they did a particular thing, the first words out of their mouth will be, "I don't know." Or sometimes we ask in our best authoritative, fatherly voice, "What were you thinking?" The answer is the same, "I don't know." Insight gives us clarity and confidence and it serves as an antidote for decisions made out of desperation and for fools who masquerade as friends.

Following shrewdness is the word *inexperienced* or *simple*. Its implication is one that is teachable and open-minded. The best teacher is always the best student. As fathers, we are to be open to the truths of the Bible, and once embraced, these truths never become negotiable. God's word is the final authority on all subjects it addresses. His word is the endless source of wisdom for building a marriage and raising children.

Knowledge comes from the Hebrew verb *yadha*, "to know intimately." Solomon wanted his children to have an intimate understanding both of the things of God and the affairs of man. If our children are going to transform our culture, they must be able to apply Christian principles to secular thought. A surgeon is to have intimate knowledge of the human body before he operates. A mechanic is to have intimate knowledge of the vehicle before he repairs it. A coach is to have intimate knowledge of the sport before he coaches. Likewise, a son or daughter should have intimate knowledge of the Scriptures before they engage the culture. This awesome responsibility and great privilege of teaching our children this knowledge should be the responsibility of the father. You do not have to do this alone. You simply participate personally in helping your children obtain this *yadha* knowledge of God's word. If it were not for godly mothers, most children would receive very little instruction and training in the classroom of Christian apologetics.

Discretion is the fourth word in verse 4. The essence is to decide one's course in life. What greater challenges do our children face than choosing the right paths to walk, the right person to marry, the right vocation to enter, and above all the right Savior to follow? How many times did our children ask us the following questions: "What will I be?"; "Who will I marry?"; "Where will I live someday?"; "When will I finish school?"; "Why do I have to study so hard?"; and "How will I know the answers to all my questions?" In the midst of all the question marks stands an exclamation point—God's word!

The words *young man* refer to being immature. All children and teenagers are immature; so are some adults called parents. At the right time, green fruit ripens. Then it is picked and ready for its intended purpose—to provide nourishment to those who eat it. In the same way, an immature child who matures will be a source of nourishment and inspiration for all who come under their influence. A fruit that never ripens, or a child who never matures, leaves a bad taste in everyone's mouth.

Dads, when you feel like a worm on the hook and the bass is about to swallow you whole, just remember who is holding the rod and reel. God and his word will provide wisdom, instruction, understanding, and knowledge when nothing else will. Verses 2, 3, and 4 are so important for sailing through Proverbs. Grasp these key words and the journey will be a breeze.

Choosing Wrong Friends

Did your father ever tell you, "You are known by the company you keep?" My father repeated this to me time and time again and guess what? Dad was right every time. I remember once in junior high school, I had a friend who was always getting into trouble. Dad sat me down to talk with me about my choice of friends. At the time, I didn't like what he said, but I learned later that my friend was convicted of some crimes and was sent to what was then called reform school. Dads, we have to protect our children, and sometimes it means we have to intervene in their choice of friends. They won't like it and probably won't understand it, but time will prove you right, and your children will learn a valuable lesson.

In chapter 1, verses 10 through 19, you find the characteristics of wrong friends and the consequences of choosing them. More is required than just knowing the friends of your children; you need to know their friends' parents. Are their values the same as yours and your wife's? Do they allow things into their home that you do not permit in yours? Quite often, you will find that the kids you don't want your kids hanging with have parents you wouldn't want to associate with either.

Wrong friends have wrong intentions. Verses 11 through 14 record the words false friends use to entice their victims into a life of crime and corruption. From Solomon's day until this very minute, the end result is the same as stated in verse 19; choosing wrong friends takes away the life of its owners.

Choosing Wisdom

In a change of voice, the remainder of chapter 1 speaks as if the mother, perhaps Bathsheba, is giving advice to the children. In addition, chapters 8 and 9 begin in the feminine gender when wisdom speaks. Often the wisest words come from the lips of godly wives and mothers. In this discourse, Wisdom pleads her case and gives warning to the consequences of ignoring her counsel. Fathers, when we, or our children, refuse to listen and follow the instructions of wisdom, only desolation, destruction, distress, and desperation await us. Remember the meaning of wisdom as defined in verse 2, moral and religious intelligence.

The source of this priceless jewel is found in chapter 2, verse 6: "For the LORD gives wisdom." As she concludes her conversation with the children, the price of ignoring wisdom is sounded loud and clear. Wisdom says there will come a time when those who have ignored her will call for her, but she will not answer. The fools will search for her but not find her. A high price must be paid for low living. Fathers, we need to reinforce continually in our children's minds the need to follow the teachings of Jesus. All other books have been written for our information, but the

Bible was written for our transformation. Proverbs is the one book you need to teach from and live out in front of your family. Our children will always face choices, and our teaching them how to make those choices early in life is one of the most valuable lessons they will ever learn.

Wisdom concludes her words of counsel in verse 33 by saying, "Whoever listens to me will live securely and be free from the fear of danger." This extraordinary promise yields extraordinary results.

2

Searching for Treasure

Have you ever been on a real treasure hunt? I understand it takes determination above all else. In the face of insurmountable odds, the ones who persevere are the ones who find the treasure. Once, I was having lunch in a home when the host, who was in his late sixties, asked those of us sitting around the table if anyone enjoyed spelunking. He was asking if anyone liked crawling around in caves. The pastor, whose name was Jerry, and I immediately replied, "Yes!" He then asked if we would like to see the cave where he found treasure as a young boy. I don't remember finishing the meal. We put on some cave-crawling clothes, grabbed a couple of flashlights, and headed out in his pick-up to the back of his property. He drove straight toward a tree located on the edge of a cliff. Slamming on the brakes, he jumped out and shouted with the excitement of a treasure seeker, "This is it." He reached down at the base of a tree, pulled up an old rope, tied it around his waist, and disappeared over the side of the bluff.

Jerry and I stood there in stunned silence. A moment later, we heard, "Come on down." As we peered over the side of what looked like the Grand Canyon, I yelled down, "We'll pray for you." His voice coming out of the side of the cliff responded, "Don't need prayer. Just tie the rope around your waist and come on down." By this time, Jerry and I were praying for the rapture. I told Jerry, "If this elderly gentleman can climb down the face of this cliff so can we." He had this blank stare on his face like, "We're going to die." While Jerry was reciting the Lord's Prayer, I pulled up the rope, tied it around my waist, and eased myself off the ledge. Fifty feet into my descent, I suddenly found myself hanging in front of a huge cave opening. My host smiled and said, "Swing on in." When I dropped beside him, I then realized Jerry was still up top probably running back to the house. I yelled, "Piece of cake, come on down!" We heard this quivering voice ask, "Are you sure?" Moments later, Jerry dropped in, and the three of us began our expedition. About one hundred yards into this hole in the earth, I looked backed over my shoulder; the opening that had been so large moments before looked smaller than the face of my flashlight. We made a left-hand turn and started down a tunnel that narrowed into a funnel. Then our Indiana Jones host said, "Boys, we've got to get on our bellies and crawl for just a bit." By this time, I'm thinking if Becky knew where I was and what I was doing, she would call our life insurance agent to tell him to cash in my policy.

Just then, he stopped and stated, "Turn out your lights." I thought, "We're in here with a serial killer and no one will ever find our bodies." Jerry exclaimed,

"Say what?" I reached up and grabbed "Indy's" ankle. If I fell in a hole, he was going with me. Then I felt Jerry's hand around my ankle, and I knew he was thinking the same thing. We turned off our flashlights, and darkness doesn't begin to describe what engulfed us. My mind recalled every word to express what I was experiencing: coal-black, jet-black, pitch-black, ebony, raven, inky darkness, and black hole. The darkness, combined with the dampness of the cave, was so intense it clung to my skin like a wet shirt. The sound of our guide's voice broke my momentary mental free fall: "Crawl up here beside me." I worked my hand up his back with Jerry doing the same to me. When I touched his shoulder, he said, "Stop!" By this time, I could taste the blackness of this cavern, and my eyes were bigger than the cave entrance.

He said boys, "Tell me what you hear." I couldn't hear anything except my heart pounding in my ears. Then I heard the faint noise of water rushing over rocks. He continued, "Turn on your lights." When we clicked on our flashlights, we were looking straight down a 150-foot drop off. Silence! I could hardly speak. Finally, I asked a brilliant question, "What's down there?" A boyish grin crept across this gentleman's face, and he said, "People who didn't stop when I told them to." Then he laughed and told us he and some of his friends had found treasure at the bottom of this cliff when they were kids.

As I shined my flashlight around this precipice, I saw an old rope ladder hanging by a few strands leading down to a pool of water being fed by an internal waterfall. He said there had always been stories about how the Indians had lived in that cave and had left behind an abundance of priceless artifacts. He said he and his friends explored the cave with lanterns and twine so they wouldn't get lost. When they came to the spot where the three of us were lying, they decided to build the rope ladder and climb down. He pointed to the bottom near the waterfall and said, "There is where we found the treasure." And find it they did. They discovered arrowheads, spears, jewelry, pottery, and ceremonial headdresses. So important was the find that the state later purchased the land and preserved it as a historical site in memory of the Native Americans who had explored the darkness long before us. I was truly in the presence of a real-life Indiana Jones. He didn't give up until he had found the treasure.

Fathers, we have a treasure far more valuable and longer lasting than what was found in the cave. Jesus said those who follow him will have a home in heaven that is like a treasure so valuable all that a man might possess cannot compare to it. In Luke 12:34, he also said, "For where your treasure is, there your heart will be also." Let me ask you as a father, "What do you treasure most on this earth?" Whatever it is controls your heart. Once again, the words of Jesus echo through history with as much authority today as when they fell from his lips: "Don't collect for yourselves treasures on earth, where moth and rust destroys and where thieves break in and steal.

But collect for yourselves treasures in heaven, where neither moth nor rust destroys, and where thieves don't break in and steal" (Matt. 6:19-20).

One of the greatest gifts you can ever give your children is a GPS (God's Positioning System). Where we came from, why we are here, and where we are going is all found in this GPS treasure map called the Bible. Just as my friend and his buddies explored every cavern in the cave until they found the earthly treasure, you as a father are to take your children through every passage of Holy Scripture so they can find the heavenly treasure. The best legacy to leave your children is to have been their guide in their search for the greatest treasure of all.

Source of Wisdom

Verse 6 of chapter 2 is the nucleus of every spiritual cell, and I might add physical as well. Without the wisdom of God and his creative powers, there would be no unity in the physical universe. Without the wisdom of God in the moral and religious realm, there would be no goodness and rightness in the spirit of man. This wisdom cannot be given by a politician, educator, philosopher, scientist, or theologian. Neither does this wisdom come from past religious leaders such as Confucius, Buddha, Zoroaster, or Muhammad. Only one source for true wisdom exists, and it is found in the one who told Moses his name is, "I AM WHO I AM" (Exod. 3:14).

We as fathers are often the ones our children look to for all the answers. If we assume this role, we undertake the role of God. We need to take our children to the Scriptures when they come to us with the issues of life. We do not have all the answers, but the Word of God never misleads, misinforms, misguides, or misdirects. What we do not understand empirically we teach them to accept by faith because God is the source of true wisdom. Christian husbands and fathers should consider it imperative to take time every day to open this treasure chest with their families and examine the priceless riches found within it. Surveys have found that 90 percent of fathers who claim to be born again do not read the Bible with their families on a daily basis. What loving father would allow his children to go a day without physical nourishment? Yet, millions of fathers who call themselves born-again Christians are spiritually starving their children on a regular basis. Our children cannot transform the culture in which they live and move without knowing the source of wisdom and more importantly without a personal relationship with the giver of wisdom.

Verse 7 tells us that God stores up sound wisdom for the upright or righteous person. The phrase "stores up" comes from the Hebrew word *caphan*, meaning "to lay up, to hide as one hides a treasure." So, here again we must dig for the nuggets of truth in Holy Scripture. But be assured, if you dig, you will discover the wisdom for which you are seeking. The Bible tells us,

> Now if any of you lacks wisdom, he should ask of God, who gives to all generously and without criticizing, and it will be given to him. But let him ask in faith not doubting. For the doubter is like the surging sea, driven and tossed by the wind. That person should not expect to receive anything from the Lord. An indecisive man is unstable in all his ways" (James 1:5-8).

"Sound wisdom" refers to stability. If there is

anything children and teenagers need in their lives, it is a stable family. The number one fear of children is abandonment from their parents. Over one million children are victims of divorce each year. Divorce turns their world upside down and inside out. They go from being the center of the family to being on the outside watching at least one parent become focused on their own desires to the neglect of everyone else. Building your marriage and your family around the principles found in God's word is one of the best ways to ensure stability in an unstable world. We as fathers cannot always be present to guard our children from taking the wrong paths or making the wrong choices. We cannot always rescue them before they enter a crisis or before they become involved in destructive relationships. This would emotionally cripple them and leave them totally dependent on us. Our children must learn from our examples that God alone is their protector and provider.

He will lead them in the paths of right conduct into a way of life that is on the level and full of righteousness. Our responsibility is to live before them what we want to leave behind after we are gone.

Characteristics of the Wicked

Have you ever had one of your teenage children ask you why they can't hang out with another teenager or a particular group of teens? All parents face this question. The answer can be as simple as, "Because I have gone down that road and let me tell you what happened," or as insightful as, "Let me share with you the characteristics of those who practice wickedness and then you decide." Whichever response you choose, you would be wise to use this teachable moment to take your children to the Scriptures.

Solomon observed five major distinctive features of those who practice evil in chapter 2, verses 12 through 15. First, they speak perverse things. Wicked people have their own language. They may be refined or rough, but either way their limited vocabulary is repulsive. Perverse speech is so common in our culture that very few television programs can be viewed longer than a minute without hearing some deviant dialogue. Like lava from an erupting volcano, vulgar speech spews forth from the mouth of the wicked.

Second, they walk in the ways of darkness. Everyone has a choice regarding the path they walk, even if the right choice means death. The wicked come to the fork in the road and choose to take the way of darkness and destruction. Those who travel on this shadowy road wear the sinister shroud of deception. They talk of being full and living the good life when, in reality, they are empty and homeless according to verse 22.

Third, the only satisfaction they experience is in the wicked lifestyle they practice. Fathers, we need to teach our children that evil has an infectious power greater than that of holiness. Less effort is required to engage black-hearted deeds than those of virtue. The Christian will always be in a spiritual battle between the flesh and the spirit. In the case of the wicked, the battle is seldom recognized. They eagerly march to the orders of the prince of darkness. Titus 1:15 contrasts the godly with the godless: "To the pure, everything is pure, but to those who are defiled and unbelieving nothing is pure; in fact, both their mind and conscience are defiled."

Fourth, much truth is contained in the adage, "You are known by the company you keep." Good people associate with those who practice goodness. Wicked people associate with those who practice wickedness. Verse 14 tells us a major characteristic of the wicked is that they rejoice in doing evil. They not only boast about their lifestyle, but also they keep company with others who do the same. Knowing who your children call friends is vitally important if for no other reason than this. I have counseled with numerous parents who relate the same story only in different terms. Their son or daughter got into the wrong crowd and proceeded to take their first steps into the dark side. Wicked friends can begin with a clique at school that surfs the Internet, or it can take place, believe it or not, in a church group that majors on games rather than growth. Fathers, you not only have the right, but also the obligation to know your children's friends and the parents of these friends. No one should care more for your children than you.

Fifth, and perhaps the most conspicuous characteristic of wicked people, is their way of life is always corrupt and criminal. They are crafty and deceitful in every decision they make and every sentence they utter. Solomon says, "Their ways are devious." I am sure we have all encountered more than one person who fits this profile. Unscrupulous and dishonest people have no integrity and prey on those who do. Dads, teach your children to ask God for the ability to discern the intentions of others.

Characteristics of the Immoral Woman

Verses 16 through 19 give us a glimpse of a father talking to his sons about the "birds and the bees," so to speak. Solomon warns his sons to avoid the immoral or forbidden woman. The meaning is clear. Stay away from any woman whose life is devoid of virtue. She may be a prostitute or a professor. She may sing in nightclubs or the church choir. She will appear sincere, but sin has its root in her heart.

The classic example of such a woman is Delilah. She used flattering words while setting Samson up for a fatal fall. She professed love for him while possessing a heart of greed. The devious ways of the wicked are eventually exposed, but often too late for the victim.

The woman mentioned here in Proverbs made a choice to forsake her upbringing, the Abrahamic Covenant. She knew the teachings of God, but she chose to walk the crooked path. Maybe she had been married and became enticed and entangled in the web of sexual pleasures. Fathers, teach your children that while they are free to choose, they are not free not to choose, and they are not free to choose the consequences of their choices. Every choice, good or bad, has a consequence. One wrong decision can affect an individual for the rest of their life. Thank

God, for he can and will forgive us our sins and hold them against us no more. However, a high price must be paid for low living, and that price might be a lifetime of physical disease or even death.

Some time ago, a story appeared in a national magazine. The article was about a very successful businessman who traveled to New York City for a high-powered business meeting. After checking into a five-star hotel, he requested a high-priced call girl be sent to his room for the night. When he awoke the next morning, the seductress had taken her money and returned to her lair. She did, however, leave one thing behind. She left him a note. When he turned on the bathroom light, the words, "WELCOME TO THE WORLD OF AIDS!" were written on the mirror in her lipstick. Needless to say, his world came to a paralyzing halt. When his doctor confirmed he was HIV positive, the businessman had to face his wife and children. Through a series of events, a staff writer from a magazine contacted him and asked permission to print his story without using his name. The story was written not to teach a moral lesson, but to inform promiscuous men to use protection.

Let me say to all husbands and fathers that the lesson in this story is this: Don't be promiscuous! Teach your children that sexual purity before marriage and sexual faithfulness after marriage is the best protection for a clear conscience and a healthy body. The woman mentioned in this chapter offers neither to those who take the path to her house. The fact is none return who go to her house. The words of Solomon still ring true some three thousand years later: "At the end of your life you will lament when your physical body has been consumed." What a chilling reminder of the high price of low living.

3

Future

Solomon begins the third chapter of Proverbs by telling his son not to forget the law he has passed down to him. His father, King David, had passed down the same law to him. The commandment of God is called the Shema. You will find it in Deuteronomy 6:4-9:

> Listen, Israel: The LORD our God is One. Love the LORD your God with all your heart, with all your soul, and with all your strength. These words I am giving you today are to be in your heart. Repeat them to your children. Talk about them when you sit in your house and when you walk along the road, when you lie down and when you get up. Bind them as a sign on your hand and let them be a symbol on your forehead. Write them on the doorposts of your house and on your gates.

Solomon was telling his children that God's laws are to be exhibited in open confession and private conviction. Head knowledge without heart knowledge offers intelligence without compassion. The greatest weapon against the enemies of your children is the Word of God hidden in their hearts.

Three themes appear in this chapter. The first deals

with the future of your children. In verses 5 and 6, the formula is given to answer all the "What should I be when I grow up?" questions. How many times have you heard your child say, "When I get big I'm going to be a . . ."? If you had asked me when I was in the fourth grade what I was going to be when I grew up, I would have answered, "A doctor!" When I was twelve years old, I promised God in a youth service at the Baptist assembly in Ridgecrest, North Carolina, that I would do anything he wanted me to do but be a preacher. My father was a preacher, and I thought one in the family was enough. I did not mind being a preacher's kid, but I was going to be a doctor. I read medical books throughout junior high and high school. One of my majors in college was biology. I did not have a 4.0 grade point average, but I had a passion for medicine. With only two months to go before graduation, I came down with a case of the miseries. Something inside was churning like the seas before the hurricane. I told God one morning on the way to my English literature class that I had to have some relief. I couldn't concentrate. I couldn't sleep. I couldn't get any peace about applying to medical school. Then the Holy Spirit took me back to that night when I was twelve in the old auditorium in Ridgecrest. I saw myself walking the aisle saying, "I'll do anything you want me to do but be a preacher." At that point, God spoke to me, "I do not work with conjunctions." I knew immediately what God was whispering into my life and heart. *And, because, but,* and *unless* are conjunctions. I had told God anything *but*. With God, you surrender either all or nothing at all. I knew I had to remove the conjunction from my promise in order for him to fulfill his promises to me. Instead of enrolling in medical school that fall, I entered the Southern Baptist Theological Seminary and eventually earned a doctor of ministry from Golden Gate Baptist Theological Seminary rather than a doctor of medicine. God's ways are always the best. He knows our strengths and weaknesses.

The heavenly Father knows our children better than we earthly fathers do. When your little boy or girl crawls in your lap and asks, "What will I be when I grow up?" take them to verses 5 and 6. "Trust in the LORD with all your heart, and do not rely on your own understanding; think about Him in all your ways, and He will guide you on the right paths."

Finances

The second theme of chapter 3 is finances. Perhaps the most difficult area to manage in the life of a young adult is the financial. If your children are out of the nest and flying, or at least hopping on their own, then making ends meet is a top priority for them. We taught our children the principle of tithing as soon as they could understand the concept of money. My father did the same for me, and Becky's father taught her that the first thing out of the paycheck was the portion belonging to God. I remember asking my father if God was poor. He sat me down and taught me that not only does God own the cattle on a thousand hills, but also he owns the universe.

We are commanded to return the first-fruits of our labor as a reminder that everything comes from God. Obedience is required. If you cheat God, you cheat yourself as well. His word promises us that his blessings follow our obedience. We are told in verse 9 that if we honor the Lord with the first check from our wages, then he will meet our needs and give us an overflow of blessings. You do not have here the health-and-wealth, name-it-and-claim-it, blab-it-and-grab-it philosophy often espoused by the charlatans who use their pulpits and media ministries to twist Scripture.

The blessings of God may certainly be financial, but they may also take the form of a godly marriage, good health, obedient children, and personal contentment. These things are indeed priceless. However, if you are not practicing tithing, you cannot teach your children the biblical mandate of this time-honored principle without being hypocritical. They need to see it practiced in front of them, so they can see God honor his promises. Start them when they are young, and it will become second nature to them when they leave home.

Family Discipline

The third theme of this chapter is family discipline. Every father and mother must face this area of child development. Given the fact that more than nineteen million children in the United States live with a single parent, which is usually the mother, we have millions of children who have no consistent male authority figure in their lives. When girls do not have a father in their lives, they are 2.5 times more likely to become pregnant outside of marriage and 53 percent more likely to commit suicide. When boys do not have a father in their lives, they are twice as likely to drop out of school, twice as likely to go to jail, and nearly four times more likely to need help for emotional and behavioral problems. The absence of a father not only impedes emotional and spiritual growth, but also has a tremendous impact on the behavior of the child or children. It doesn't take a Harvard graduate to verify this truth.

Verses 11 and 12 lay the foundation for the discipline of children. First, it tells us if you are a child of God, you are to neither despise nor detest his discipline. Not everyone is part of the family of God according to Holy Scripture. Everyone is his creation, but only those who have confessed Jesus as

Lord and Savior are truly a part of the family of God. Jesus said, "I am the way, the truth, and the life. No one comes to the Father except through Me" (John 14:6). Second, verse 12 tells us, "For the LORD disciplines the one He loves, just as a father, the son he delights in." Offering one side of God's nature, 1 John 4:8 states, "God is love." Here in Proverbs we find another side, that of the disciplinarian.

Even outside of divinity, love, and correction are images on the same coin. An undisciplined child becomes a spoiled child. You don't need the Bible to convince you of this fact. But just in case, Proverbs 29:15 informs us, "The rod [physical discipline] and reproof [verbal discipline] give wisdom, but a child left to himself brings shame to his mother" (New King James Version). The phrase "left to himself" is the English equivalent of the word *spoiled*. Simply put, an undisciplined child becomes a spoiled child. And we all know the characteristics of a spoiled child. The sad result is that a spoiled child develops into a spoiled adult who marries. The bottom line is that loving discipline is a sure sign of a loving father. When you tell your child, "This is going to hurt me more than it hurts you," they will not understand it, but you will.

4

Gaining Wisdom

Three themes are the dominant focus of this chapter. The first is wisdom. As stated in verse 2 of chapter 1, "To know wisdom" is the first priority of anyone who seeks more than the mundane, commonplace journey through life. You will recall from chapter 2, verse 6 the source of wisdom. Solomon begins this lesson by calling his children to attention, "Listen, my sons, [children], to a father's discipline and pay attention so that you may gain understanding." The word *listen* in this context means "give me your eyes and ears." He then proceeds to tell them what their grandfather, King David, had taught him. A wise man once said that wisdom has four principles: the principle of rightness, the principle of integrity, the principle of courage, and the principle of contentment. The first implies that your actions and words are the same. The second is a lifestyle of honesty and noble character. The third allows you to stand for that which is right even if you stand alone. The fourth allows you to control your desires so that neither poverty nor riches turn your heart from God.

Verse 7 contains the two most valuable possessions a father can challenge his children to obtain during their days on this earth: wisdom and understanding.

Remember, wisdom means the gift of moral and religious intelligence. Understanding means intellectual intelligence. Nothing is needed more in the world than fathers, mothers, sons, and daughters who possess this priceless alloy. You will not find this treasure in the educational, political, economical, or religious institutions of higher learning. The Bible is the source of the Word of the living God. Bring both your simple childlike faith and your mental abilities to Scripture, and the Holy Spirit will be your personal tutor. A non-Christian will not be able to comprehend the truths or the depths of the Word of God outside a personal relationship with Jesus Christ. If you want your children to get into the Word of God, the Word must get into them first. Confessing Jesus Christ as their Lord and Savior is the singular most important decision your children will ever make. This one decision will have consequences for all eternity. Solomon instructed his children in verse 10, "Listen my son, accept my words and you will live many years." He knew that being able to cope with the demands and stresses of life successfully requires both wisdom and understanding. God created this combination to guide your children in their relationships throughout life. It will determine their choice of a spouse. It will chart their vocational selection. It will be their guide in raising children. It will also comfort you should your children choose a wrong path.

Avoiding Evil People

The second theme of this chapter is the contrast between evil people and good people. Solomon had plenty of opportunities to observe both kinds. In verses 14 and 15, he gives the three "Do not's." Do not enter. Do not walk. Do not travel. These three instructions pertain to running with the wrong crowd. "Do not enter the path of the wicked." Our children will be faced with many paths in their formative years. Some paths will develop them. Some paths will destroy them. That first choice to smoke it, pop it, drink it, see it, and feel it can lead down a dark, winding labyrinth of passages into a life of confusion, perplexity, and complication. We have always told our children that a true friend will never seek to either hurt you or ask you to compromise your convictions. Every father has told his children in one way or another, "You are known by the company you keep." Adam proved this true, and it will continue to be so until the last father has spoken.

Once a path is chosen, it is only natural to start walking. Someone walking with the wrong crowd will wind up in the wrong place. Solomon said, "Do not walk in the way of evil." The prodigal son entered the world of self-destruction when he took the first step out of his father's house and started walking toward the bright lights of compromise and concessions. The way of evil is very infectious. The effects are more extensive and lasting than that of holiness. A holy life requires consistent obedience to the claims of Christ. An evil life requires only obedience to the cravings of the flesh. A holy life seeks the truth. Jesus said about himself, "I am the way, the truth, and the life. No one comes to the Father except through Me" (John 14:6). Truth is always narrow. Evil is always broad. Truth is exclusive. Evil is inclusive. If you want your children taught the truth about history, math, chemistry, and all the other subjects in school, why wouldn't you want them to learn the greatest truth of all?

When the walk has begun, the traveling becomes secondary. Again, the prodigal son traveled far from home to a place where the teachings of his father were put to the test. He was free to choose, but he was not free not to choose. And he wasn't free to choose the consequences of his choices. He soon became destitute and found himself deserted. You have here the perfect picture of a person without God. The glitz, glamour, and gold of the world leaves you deceived, defeated, disillusioned, and disappointed. King Solomon warned his sons not to set foot on the path of the wicked. Sin is contagious. The effects spread like a bacterial infection. You can catch a disease, but you cannot catch health. Solomon told his sons to stay away from those who are infected with the sinful lifestyle. What great advice for us fathers to pass on to our sons and daughters.

Paying Attention

The third theme is picked up in verses 20 through 27. In these instructions, Solomon makes use of the anatomy to personalize his parental training. He said,

> Incline your *ear* to my sayings. Do not let them depart from your *eyes;* keep them in the midst of your *heart;* for they are *life* to those who find them, and *health* to all their *flesh*. Keep your *heart* with all diligence, for out of it spring the issues of *life*. Put away from you a deceitful *mouth,* and put perverse *lips* far from you. Let your *eyes* look straight ahead, and your *eyelids* look right before you. Ponder the path of your *feet,* and let all your ways be established. Do not turn to the right or the left; remove your *foot* from evil.

Nine times Solomon refers to parts of the body visible to the naked eye. Five times he mentions that which cannot been seen but is vital, nevertheless, to the overall fitness of the body. The beginning of a sound body is a sound mind. Proverbs 23:7 tells us, "For as he thinks in his heart, so is he." In Psalm 24:3-4, clean hands and a pure heart are linked together. John Phillips, a well-known Bible scholar, puts it this way, "We do what we do because we are what we are." Someone once said, "Behind what the man will do lies what the boy was thinking." Paying attention to the godly advice of a godly father will more than likely result in a godly child who will someday more than likely become a godly parent.

Many of us learned a particular song in church as children. A portion of it advises,

> Oh, be careful little ears, what you hear . . . Oh, be careful little eyes, what you see . . . Oh, be careful little mouth, what you say . . . Oh, be careful little hands, what you do . . . Oh, be careful little feet where you go . . . Oh, be careful little mind what you think . . . Oh, be careful little heart what you love. For the Father up above, is looking down in love, so be careful little heart, what you love.

Solomon is telling his children the exact same thing. Fathers, you must be careful what you take into your minds because it will surely come out in your actions. What enters our ears often enters our hearts. Most temptations come through the eyes, and it is easy for the look to become a lust. Evil words reveal an evil heart. Hands that touch the forbidden fruit corrupt the entire body. Feet that do not stay at home may end up in the pigpen. The responsibility of setting the example for your sons and daughters is the greatest challenge you will face as a father. If you pay attention to the Word of God and practice what it teaches, then you will have a clear conscience when your children raise their children to be just like their grandfather.

5

Sexual Purity

No better advice or counsel on the lifestyle of the immoral, loose, promiscuous woman will you find than what is given in chapters 5 and 7. Solomon was an observer of people. His own palace was a center of chaos and confusion, of jealousy and conspiracy, of liaisons and lust. He disobeyed God and brought pagan wives into his kingdom. They turned his heart from obedience to rebellion. Even though Solomon did not follow his own advice, what he did say is wise and worthy of adoption.

In verses 1 and 2, the theme is guard your spirit. Solomon once again tells his son to pay attention to what he is about to share with him. Dads, we need to make sure that when we speak our sons and daughters are listening. In this sound-bite generation, where we are led to believe that we must speak fast, listen fast, and eat fast, we need to slow down, especially when it comes to matters concerning our children. Solomon uses three words relating to guarding your spirit: *understanding, discretion,* and *knowledge.* Understanding means to have the intelligence to comprehend who and what is calling for your heart. In this context, discretion means your course in life, having your goals set so nothing will distract you. Knowledge means to know intimately. An in-depth knowledge of the Scriptures combined with an obedient heart can save your children from the snares waiting for them.

The theme of verses 3 through 14 is guard your body. Solomon is about to describe to his sons the physical reasons for remaining faithful to your spouse and sexually pure in the vows of marriage. He knew the approach taken by the professional harlot. Her enticing words and painted lips are only a veneer for the danger and death that lie beneath. A prostitute, paid or not, baits her trap with words smoother than oil and dripping with honey. She entices with titillating looks that arouse the sexual appetite. Yet, Solomon said that in reality, her passion is poison and her destination is death.

He warned his sons not to take the path to her dwelling. The results are numerous. First, you lose your honor or reputation. However, in the culture in which we live today, immorality is both tolerated and common place; nevertheless, sin is still sin. Second, many a husband has lost his marriage and been alienated from his children because of the smooth words and enticing looks of a woman on the prowl. Third, as Solomon warned, strangers will be filled with your wealth through either blackmail, or the sexual addiction that follows this lifestyle. Fourth, he describes the physical results that occur when promiscuous sexual behavior has taken its toll.

Sexual Disease

In Solomon's day, there were two basic types of sexually transmitted diseases (STDs): gonorrhea and syphilis. He had undoubtedly seen firsthand the final stages of syphilis and what it does to the body. Today there are more than twenty STDs in the United States. More than sixty-five million Americans have an STD that cannot be cured with medication. Included in this list are herpes, hepatitis B, and HIV. Experts estimate that about nineteen million Americans contract an STD every year. One in two of every newly diagnosed STDs infects a teenager or young adult. Teenagers and young adults are becoming infected faster than any other group in America. Each year 134,000 new cases of syphilis are occurring, the highest infection rate in forty years. New gonorrhea cases occur annually at the rate of 1.3 million. New cases of human papilloma virus occur annually at the rate of 24 million, including a high percentage among teens. The number of all STD cases occurring among people less than twenty-five years of age is 63 percent. AIDS is the leading killer of Americans between the ages of twenty-five and forty-four. However, in spite of prevention efforts, new cases of some of the most common STDs are still on the rise according to the United States Centers for Disease Control and Prevention.

Sexual Faithfulness

Dads, you need to have a face-to-face, heart-to-heart talk with your sons and daughters about this God-given gift called sex. When expressed properly in the context of a faithful marriage, sex is beautiful, fulfilling, and the highest expression of communication between a man and woman. Prostitution has been referred to as the oldest profession. But remember, marriage came first. When a husband or wife is willing to break their vows of faithfulness, severe consequences follow. In chapter 6, verse 7 Solomon stated, "The one who commits adultery lacks sense; whoever does so destroys himself." You teach your children by example.

Job 28:11 tells us that God brings to light that which is hidden. If there is any unconfessed sin in your life, know this, only Jesus can extend complete forgiveness. And when he forgives, he forgets. Psalm 103:12 says, "As far as the east is from the west, so far has He removed our transgressions from us." Anyone who confesses Jesus as Lord and Savior and turns to him for forgiveness will find this true. However, you are not licensed to continue in sin. The apostle Paul addressed this issue in his writings in Romans 6:18: "And having been liberated from sin you became enslaved to righteousness." In other words, that which frees you also enslaves you. Every one is a slave to that which drives them, challenges them, and inspires them. If you wish for your children a life of wisdom and blessings, teach them that slavery is not an antiquated word and a lifestyle to be avoided. Your children will only know freedom and fulfillment when they willfully choose to exchange their lives for his. Salvation is what it is called.

We are told in Romans 10:9-10, "If you confess with your mouth, 'Jesus is Lord,' and believe in your heart that God raised Him from the dead, you will be saved. With the heart one believes, resulting in righteousness, and with the mouth one confesses, resulting in salvation." A combination of the mind and heart is required. Have you as a father experienced salvation for yourself? If so, have you shared your experience with your children?

The theme of verses 15 through 20 is guard your marriage. Solomon uses the language of the poets to underscore the importance of the sexual relationship between husband and wife. He speaks of "drinking water from your own well," meaning that sexual pleasures are to be experienced at home. The word *fountain* is to be translated as "your own wife." This principle of fidelity in marriage needs to be taught to your sons and daughters. Sex is a vital piece of the puzzle called marriage. If you leave this piece out or neglect it, you will never know the joy of intimacy at its most profound level.

Surveys and questionnaires today show that fathers do not talk to their sons about sexual matters anymore than their fathers talked to them. Your children are bombarded with sexual images with every waking hour. The Internet is now the leading supplier of pornography in the world. On January 21, 2009, in the case of the *ACLU* v. *Mukasey,* the United States Supreme Court refused to revive the Child Online Protection Act, an act designed to protect children from sexual material and other objectionable content on the Internet. The Supreme Court has defined four categories of pornography that can be determined illegal. Illegal pornography includes indecency, material harmful to minors, obscenity, and child pornography. The high court decided not to restore the federal law that would have required Web sites featuring harmful content to minors to put in place measures that prevent minors from viewing the site. However, the Justice Department will continue to prosecute producers and adult consumers of pornography. Talk about a paradox. You can prohibit an adult from buying pornography, but you can't prohibit an adult from giving it to a child at least over the Internet.

As long as your children are at home, the computers in the house need to be in full view at all times. All passwords should be available to every family member. Dads, you shouldn't view anything on your computer that you wouldn't want your son or daughter to view. Sit down with your children while they are watching their favorite television programs and count the number of times sexual images are used directly and indirectly to influence their choice of a product. Check the number of times a sexual theme is used to market what you purchase. Sex sells. It not only sells, but it also stimulates. It not only stimulates, but it also entices. It not only entices, but it also calls for action. The advice of Solomon is helpful at this point. He told his children not to enter, walk, or travel on the path that leads to destruction. When my wife is addressing teenage girls and young women, she informs them that fifteen minutes of sexual pleasure outside of marriage can lead to a lifetime of regret. The same holds true for our sons. Solomon ends chapter 5 with these words, "For the ways of man are before the eyes of the Lord, and He ponders all his paths."

6

Avoiding Surety

Solomon moves from instructing his sons about sexual purity to other issues they will face in their vocations. In verses 1 through 5, he begins by telling them to avoid surety. He tells his son, "If you have put up security for your neighbor or entered into an agreement with a stranger, you have been trapped by the words of your lips—ensnared by the words of your mouth." Today, we call that cosigning a note. You guarantee to pay the debt if the debtor defaults. At this point, it appears that only a verbal agreement had been made. A rash decision was made impulsively. Fathers, we need to teach our sons that financial expertise is vital for them now and in the future. Many an individual, out of a good heart, has signed a note for a friend or relative and ended up losing both.

Financial education, like spiritual training, should begin at home. As soon as your children understand the basics of 2 + 2, teach them the principle of price and purchase. Almost everything we purchase has a price measured in dollars and cents. Give your son or daughter an allowance, and when they ask for some particular item let them pay for part or all of it. Then when their allowance runs out for the week, do not give them an advance on next week's allowance. You will help them establish the financial principles they will carry with them throughout life.

Solomon with all his riches understood the need to avoid surety. He said if you have cosigned a note for someone go and ask to be released from your commitment. If your friend is truly a friend, he will understand and later thank you for keeping him and you from making a mistake. Better to save a friendship through common sense and sound financial practices than to see it dissolve in anger and hard feelings.

Avoiding Slothfulness

Secondly, Solomon tells his sons to avoid slothfulness in verses 6 through 11. In other words, do not be lazy, indolent, or idle. One of the greatest injustices a father can do to his children is to fail to teach them a strong work ethic. About the only work many children do is the working of their fingers playing video games. The prevalence of obesity among children aged six to eleven has more than doubled in the past twenty years. The rate among adolescents aged twelve to nineteen more than tripled. Many reasons are given for this, but two are at the top of the list—lack of exercise and video games. Give your children certain responsibilities and expect them to complete them before they head off to their computer games or text messaging. Get your children involved in some physical activity whether in their school, their church group, or an organization like the Boy Scouts or Girl Scouts. I cease to be amazed at how many parents are oblivious to the physical condition of their children. One reason is that many parents are themselves couch potatoes.

I was recently grocery shopping for my wife who was in bed sick. As I turned to go down an aisle, a father, mother, and their three teenage children were coming toward me. I froze. They would have been a monumental challenge for Weight Watchers. Their grocery carts were filled with snacks, junk food, and enough sodas to fill a small lake. Dads, it's hard to expect your children to take care of their bodies when you joke about neglecting yours. It's hard to teach a sound work ethic if you do not give your children specific chores and make them stick to them. Then when they have completed what you gave them to do, tell them they did a good job. Wrapping your arm around your son and telling him how proud you are of him will be something he will remember and repeat to your grandson.

Solomon was an observer of nature. He told his children to watch the ants. They are not slothful. They are not lazy. They work by instinct. Teach your children to work by instruction and example. The result of slothfulness is self-imposed poverty. When a person is poor because of uncontrollable circumstances, it is understandable. When a person is poor because they are not willing to work, it is inexcusable. There are millions in our country who would rather sit in the shade with their arms folded and draw a check from the government than put in an honest day's work. When a nation becomes slothful, it will soon cease to exist. The same is true for an individual. Verses 10 and 11 tell us, "A little sleep, a little slumber, a little folding of the arms to rest, and your poverty will come like a robber, your need, like a bandit."

The late Adrian Rogers, pastor of Bellevue Baptist Church in Memphis, Tennessee, put it this way:

You cannot legislate the poor into freedom by legislating the wealthy out of freedom. What one person receives without working for, another person must work for without receiving. The government cannot give to anybody anything that the government does not first take from somebody else. When half of the people get the idea that they do not have to work because the other half is going to take care of them, and when the other half gets the idea that it does no good to work because somebody else is going to get what they work for, that my dear friend, is about the end of any nation. You cannot multiply wealth by dividing it.

Avoiding the Sinner

The third thing Solomon instructs his children to avoid is the worthless sinner. He describes him and his lifestyle in verses 12 through 15. Fathers, you need to teach your sons and daughters that not every person is wicked, neither is every person good. Many men and women in the world live for violence and destruction. They never give second thought to their sinful actions. Do not teach your children to be paranoid but to be discerning in relationships with others. If you do not believe there are individuals who live to steal your children's innocence, kill them for psychopathic purposes, and destroy their lives, you have never checked out the pedophiles, drug pushers, and rapists in your city. The end of those who thrive on evil is described by Solomon when he says, "Calamity will strike him suddenly; he will be shattered instantly beyond recovery." Justice will prevail.

The sinner is profiled in verses 16 through 19. The reference to "seven things the LORD hates" is an expression implying the list is not exhaustive. First, is the proud look or arrogant eyes. A person of pride feels superior to others. Dads, teaching your children the desire to serve others is a lesson that will reap many rewards. Later in the book of Proverbs,

Solomon states, "Pride comes before destruction, and an arrogant spirit before a fall" (16:18).

Second, is a lying tongue. The first lie ever spoken was by Satan when he led a rebellion against God and the heavenly host. Jesus said about this deceiver, "He was a murderer from the beginning and has not stood in the truth, because there is no truth in him. When he tells a lie he speaks from his own nature, because he is a liar and the father of liars" (John 8:44). Truth may hurt, but it also heals.

Third, are hands that shed innocent blood. From Cain who killed his brother, Abel, to the latest unborn baby killed through abortion, innocent blood has been spilled throughout the ages.

Fourth, is a heart that plots wicked schemes. The depraved, perverted heart is seen today in the lifestyles of many. Fathers, teach your children to guard their heart. What goes in through the eyes and ears often comes out of the heart. Philippians 4:8 tells us, "Whatever is true, honorable, just, pure, lovely, and commendable, if there is any moral excellence and if there is any praise dwell on these things."

Fifth, are feet eager to run to evil. How many times have you told your children, "You are known by the company you keep?" That saying is so true. If you run with the dogs, you will end up barking like the dogs. If you run with the rebellious crowd, you will end up in a far country away from home. Fathers, it is a necessity to know with whom your children run and where they are running. I stood in the palatial home of a husband and wife in Nashville, Tennessee, a few years ago. Inside their foyer hung a portrait of two handsome young men. When I asked if they were their two sons, the father immediately begin to weep. He told a tragic story of how both of his sons were killed in an automobile accident just a mile from their home. His boys had been running with the wrong crowd, and one fateful night, they ran for the last time. All those in the car died as the odor of alcohol filtered around their lifeless bodies. This father will never be the same.

The sixth thing the Lord hates is a lying witness who gives false testimony. Jesus endured those who betrayed him during his last hours before the Crucifixion. Many false witnesses came forward to testify against Jesus, but none of their claims proved true. Your children will encounter false witnesses before they leave kindergarten. The pain is especially hurtful to them when they are in junior high school. They are trying to be cool, fit in, and feel good about themselves at this stage in their lives. When an individual or a group tells a lie about your child, the inward pain is tremendous. Use such an event to tell your child how you felt when this happened to you. Also, let them know that false witnesses will always be around. Those easily swayed by the words of others will always be in the shadows. Teach your children that truth will prevail even though it may be a long time coming. When integrity is maintained, it is easier to face the false witnesses the next day.

Finally, in this list, the Lord hates the one who stirs up trouble among brothers. You will always have a Cain who is jealous of Abel, an Ishmael who stands against Isaac, and an Esau in conflict with Jacob. Teaching your children to sew the seeds of peace rather than discord will reap a bountiful harvest for them throughout every area of their lives. Again, I say, our lessons to our children are better caught than taught.

Avoiding Immorality

Solomon returns to the theme of avoiding immoral behavior in verses 24 through 29. He told his sons that his commands and the teachings of their mother will protect them when they face the temptations of the wayward woman who seeks to destroy their very lives. The king reminds his sons that the godly instructions they were receiving should be bound on their hearts and worn around their necks. After all, the heart is the seat of our emotions. How many destructive decisions have been made when the heart overruled the head? A necklace is obviously worn for its beauty and is a reminder to the observer that the individual wearing it is making a statement. Solomon wanted his sons to understand that when friends and strangers saw them their very appearance would make a statement as to their character and integrity. Fathers, you owe it to your sons to teach them that as they progress in life there will always be a woman seeking to seduce them like the one described in these verses. At one time in our nation, prostitution and adultery were spoken of in hushed tones. Both are now approved, affirmed, and applauded by the media and the movies. We have politicians whose sexual liaisons have elevated them in the eyes of the public and profited them in their memoirs. When the siren seductress lures pastors, evangelists, and other religious leaders, the consequences are immeasurable. When carnal pleasures are substituted for godly standards, defeat is not far away. Morality, virtue, integrity, and honor are sacrificed when one allows the seductive, flattering tongue and the sensual, lustful look to lead from temptation to action. Solomon is so emphatic as to tell his sons in verse 32, "Whoever commits adultery with a woman lacks understanding; he who does so destroys his own soul" (NKJV). These are penetrating words spoken plainly to our promiscuous culture.

7

The Parents' Path of Life

This chapter resounds with the common thread running through the entire tapestry of Proverbs, the influence of the parents on the lives of their children. Solomon's instructions to his children, especially his sons, had a sense of urgency. Fathers, while you can command obedience in your homes, you cannot impart holiness into your children. Only God can do that, and then it must be at their personal invitation. As I often say to parents in our Hope for the Home Conferences, "All you can do is all you can do. But, be sure you do all you can." The time will come when your son or daughter will make their own choices, as well they should. I share a formula with students when I speak to them. The formula is this: *You are free to choose. You are not free not to choose. And you are not free to choose the consequences of your choices.* Solomon was saying this in verses 1 through 4:

My son, obey my words, and treasure my commands. Keep my commands and live; protect my teachings as you would the pupil of your eye. Tie them to your fingers; write them on the tablet of your heart. Say to wisdom, "You are my sister," and call understanding your relative.

Solomon knew there would be consequences to every choice his children made. He used the words *obey, treasure, keep, protect, tie,* and *write* because he knew it would require everything he had ever taught them for them to choose the right path in a world offering countless alternatives.

Your children are being faced with choices every day at school, at work, on that date, and at play. They may take a detour from the path you have taught them to walk. However, if you have lived before them what you tried to instill in them, they will likely return to their parents' path of life. Before Solomon concludes his basic instructions, he once again returns to the theme of sexual conduct.

The Seductress's Path of Death

Verses 6 through 27 are a vivid account of a story of seduction. Once again, Solomon brings up the subject of sexual immorality to his children. With his seven hundred wives and three hundred concubines, he was well qualified to address this subject. However, as it states in 1 Kings 11:3, "His wives turned his heart away from the LORD." His first wife was an Egyptian princess who undoubtedly brought her foreign gods into the marriage. His son, Rehoboam, had Naamah for a mother who was from the Ammonites. Her people worshiped the god Milcom, to whom small children were offered in sacrifice. As I shared in the beginning, Solomon's counsel and advice to his children are worthy of emulation by all fathers. The tragedy is that he did not follow his own teachings. Solomon shares his observations of a young man who fell prey to the persuasion of a seductress.

I want you to notice the ten stages of descent in the art of seduction. First, he was in the wrong place. Verse 8 states, "Crossing the street near her corner, he strolled down the road to her house at twilight, in the evening in the dark of night." The word *road* here means "back road." This seductress lived just off the main road, where she could view her prey from her house. Solomon, instead of warning the young man, watched the seduction unfold.

Second, he chose the wrong path. He deliberately made the choice to walk by her place of business. The sun was going down, and the last rays of light were turning into the deepening shades of night. Jesus said, "This, then, is the judgment: the light has come into the world, and people loved darkness rather than the light because their deeds were evil" (John 3:19). Beware of walking into the gray areas and on the gray paths. One more step and darkness surrounds you.

Third, he met the wrong person. Verse 10 describes her: "A woman came to meet him dressed like a prostitute, having a hidden agenda." The lady of the evening was dressed for the occasion. The seductress knows how to bait the trap. Catching his gaze, she turned his look into lust. The bold, frontal attack was used rather than another of her deployments in her arsenal of seductive schemes. Verse 13 says, "She grabs him and kisses him." Fathers, you need to warn your sons that being in the wrong place, choosing the wrong path, and meeting the wrong person will have devastating consequences as this young man is about to find out.

Fourth, in this descent of seduction, the adulterer sounded pious. In verse 14, we hear her say, "I have made my fellowship offerings; today I fulfilled my vows." Her logic was to pay now and sin later. She felt entitled to her night of adultery since she had paid for her indulgence earlier in the day.

Fifth, in verse 15, she sounded personal: "So, I came out to meet you, to search for you, and I have found you." She made him feel as if he was the only one she wanted. Everyone has the need to be loved and wanted. The problem arises when, as the country song said, you go looking for love in all the wrong places. This young man was being set up for a let down.

Sixth, she sounded provocative. Looking into his eyes, she said, "I have spread my coverings on my bed-richly colored linen from Egypt. I have perfumed my bed with myrrh, aloes and cinnamon. Come let's drink deeply of love making until morning. Let's feast on each other's love" (16-18). Luring him with words of seduction, she described her bedroom and its preparation just for him. She was no cheap street-walker. She had the finest furnishings and the most sensuous fragrances on the market. By this time, her sight, her speech, and her scent had already intoxi-cated the young man.

Seventh, she sounded persuasive. Taking "no" for an answer was not an option. Betraying her husband was not given a second thought. Undoubtedly, this was not the first time she had filled the role of wayward wife. Tempting him, she said, "My husband isn't home; he went on a long journey. He took a bag of money with him and will come home at the time of the full moon." With a few other sighs and enticing words, she brings him to the front door. With one last tantalizing whisper, she opens the door and his fate is sealed.

Eighth, the sensual siren delivered death. The final three stages of seduction are about to unfold in lightning speed. The night passed. The morning broke. The young man looked in the mirror and saw someone else looking back. He will never be the same. He had slept with another man's wife. He was branded an adulterer. Though sins can be forgiven only through Jesus, the memories are pressed between the pages of the mind. As has been said, "Sin takes you farther than you want to go, keeps you longer than you want to stay, and costs you more than you ever wanted to pay." The Scriptures say about this young man's decision: "He follows her impulsively like an ox going to the slaughter, like a deer bounding toward a trap until an arrow pierces its liver, like a bird darting into a snare, he doesn't know it will cost him his life" (22-23). Death was not immediate, but it was inevitable.

Ninth, the wife who played the whore delivered doom. When one is doomed, the future is grim and a terrible fate awaits the victim. One last time, Solomon pleads with his sons to listen to his counsel. He said, "Now my sons listen to me, and pay attention to the words of my mouth. Don't let your heart turn aside to her ways; don't stray onto her paths. For she has brought many down to death; her victims are countless" (24-26). How many times have we as fathers pleaded with our children to listen? How many times did our fathers plead with us? The old adage "what goes around comes around" is so true. The wisdom Solomon imparted to his sons is what millions of loving fathers have done in every culture for thousands of years. Some sons listen. Some sons do not. As stated earlier, all you can do is all you can do. But be sure you do all you can and live what you teach.

Tenth, the temptress delivered destruction. Verse 27 leaves no doubt as to the outcome of those who fall prey to the seduction of the wayward woman: "Her house is the road to Sheol, descending to the chambers of death." She traffics in desire, disease, and death. The result is destruction of the soul. A life spent on the pleasures of life will bring no pleasure in the end. Behind the attire of the adulterer lies deception. Behind her lies are broken promises. Behind her door rests the company of the dead. Behind her bedchamber lurks the cavernous mouth of hell. Many make light of the mention of Satan, hell, and eternal damnation. I can promise you that Satan never makes light of you. He takes his evil nature seriously.

As a father, you have the most significant, critical, and pivotal responsibility conceivable, raising your sons and daughters to live godly in an ungodly world. The task is daunting. The challenge is daily. The undertaking is draining. The outcome is worth it all. In those moments when you think you are the worst father of all, do not believe it. We are not perfect earthly fathers, but we can seek guidance and counsel from the heavenly Father who is perfect. His word tells us in James 1:5, "Now if any of you lacks wisdom, he should ask God, who gives to all generously and without criticizing, and it will be given him."

Epilogue

Guide for Timely Topics

Three themes reoccur throughout Proverbs that speak to the essentials of child rearing. I have addressed these in the previous chapters. The following verses and comments are given for a quick reference and biblical insight into these themes.

Integrity

Integrity is the cornerstone of all that is right, noble, and high in character in a civilized society. The value of it increases when you lose everything to keep it. Integrity comes from those who are honest, sound from center to circumference, condemn wrong in friend or foe and especially in themselves and who are devout in their dealings, earnest in their expectations, genuine in their relations, and pure in their motives. Fathers, teach your sons and daughters that individuals of integrity will stand for the right even if they must stand alone. They neither brag nor run. They have courage without bragging about it and strength without abusing it. They know their convictions and speak them without fear of rejection. They know their positions of authority and fill them without compromise. They are trustworthy. One is never poor when integrity fills his heart. Integrity is slowly developed but can be quickly lost. Teach your children that at all costs they must guard their hearts.

Proverbs 10:9: *"The one who lives with integrity lives securely, but whoever perverts his ways will be found out."* In the world in which we live, very few things are secure. A father who teaches his children integrity by example is a wise father.

Proverbs 20:11: *"Even a young man is known by his actions by whether his behavior is pure and upright."* The actions of a young man will likely be repeated as an adult. Someone once said, "Behind what the man will do lies what the boy was thinking."

Proverbs 23:15: *"My son, if your heart is wise, my heart will indeed rejoice."* A wise heart reveals a son whose mind is fixed on the things of God.

Proverbs 23:19-21: *"Listen my son, and be wise; keep your mind on the right course. Don't associate with those who drink too much wine, or with those who gorge themselves on meat. For the drunkard and the glutton will become poor, and grogginess will clothe them in rags."* Choosing the right course requires integrity and commitment; both are learned in childhood.

Proverbs 23:24: *"The father of a righteous son will delight in him."* Nothing brings more pride to a father than to have a godly son, assuming the father is also godly.

Proverbs 27:19: *"As the water reflects the face, so the heart reflects the person."* When one looks into still water, he sees a reflection of himself and not another. When one looks at his actions, he is looking into his own heart and not that of another. Distorted mirrors like distorted hearts disfigure the reflection of the possessor. The heart of health is a healthy heart beating in the body of integrity. Looking into a mirror is easy if the person looking back is one of integrity.

Discipline

The order of discipline in the home should fall on the shoulders of the father and not the mother. Yet, in the United States, we have at present more than nineteen million children who live with a single parent. In the majority of these cases, the mother, not the father, raises and disciplines the child or children. When Plato once saw a child misbehaving, he corrected the father. How appropriate that is for today. Fewer sons and daughters would need disciplining if their fathers were both present and accountable. The best way for a father to discipline his children is for him to be a disciplined man. The first thing a father should do each morning before the family goes off in different directions is have at least one verse of Scripture and a prayer with everyone present. This simple example will do more to deter the need for physical discipline than you can imagine. Discipline begins the moment you realize that your child is not perfect. Usually, that is about a week after they are born. Just as the fruits of trees grow up with the trees, so the limbs do not break under the weight of the fruit, so do the fruits of loving discipline grow up with a child. The choicest fruit of a child is obedience. The second is respect. These two should be followed with the teachings of Holy Scripture, which will in turn produce fruit that only God's word can harvest.

Proverbs 12:1: *"Whoever loves instruction loves knowledge, but one who hates correction is stupid."* How much more direct can you get? The conjunction *but* is used by Solomon in Proverbs like a metronome. The regularly repeated tick calls to attention the contrasts between light and darkness, right and wrong, good and evil, discipline and rebellion.

Proverbs 13:18: *"Poverty and disgrace come to those who ignore instruction, but the one who accepts rebuke will be honored."* Two things are promised to the person who will not accept discipline. Financial poverty is not the worst thing a person can encounter; however, poverty of character is. Disgrace comes to those who think they are above the law and beneath the protection of its judgment. Honor comes to the one who has submitted to discipline from childhood. The makeup of one's heart and not the opinions of others is the cornerstone of honor.

Proverbs 13:24: *"The one who will not use the rod hates his son, but the one who loves him disciplines him diligently."* The word *rod* implies physical discipline. This verse is not encouraging abuse, just the opposite. If a father loves his children, he will discipline them out of love, not hatred. An undisciplined child becomes a spoiled child, and a spoiled child becomes a spoiled adult.

Proverbs 15:5: *"A fool despises his father's instruction, but a person who heeds correction is sensible."* A fool is one who lacks sense or judgment. Many a godly father has had a son who played the part of a fool. Take heed fathers; your godly instructions will always be a testimony to your faithfulness. The truth is that godly parents can have foolish children. King Hezekiah and his wife Hephzibah are perfect examples of this. Their son, Manasseh, had no excuse for his evil actions as recorded in 2 Kings 21. If godly parents can have foolish children, the opposite is also true. Foolish parents can have godly children. Only through God's divine intervention in the lives of the children will this happen.

Proverbs 15:10: *"Discipline is harsh for the one who leaves the path; the one who hates correction will die."* The headstrong, hard-hearted, openly defiant son or daughter is often disciplined by death. Sad but true.

Proverbs 15:32: *"Anyone who ignores instruction despises himself, but whoever listens to correction acquires good sense."* Here you have the formula I shared earlier. You are free to choose. You are not free not to choose. You are not free to choose the consequences or your choice. You may have one child who lives to break the rules and another who lives to follow the rules.

Proverbs 19:18: *"Discipline your son while there is hope; don't be intent on killing him."* Today, the "experts" would have you believe that discipline is a thing of the past and that self-assertiveness is the norm. This verse implies that without discipline you might actually be an accomplice to your child's death. I often speak in jails and prisons. The one thread running through every place of incarceration is the absence of fathers during the formative years of the inmates. No fathers. No discipline.

Proverbs 22:15: *"Foolishness is tangled up in the heart of a youth; the rod of discipline will drive it away from him."* Again, Solomon imparts the wisdom of a parent. Do all children rebel? I guess that depends on how you define rebellion. In our home, rebellion meant going against authority, deliberately disobeying either dad or mom, or both. Some children are more rebellious than others. Some will test you to the limit and beyond. Consistency in discipline is the challenge. Sometimes parents let things slide instead of confronting the situation. However, your children need and want consistency in your lives and theirs. With so much of their world changing everyday, it is reassuring to them to know that their father's love and discipline are constant.

Proverbs 29:15: *"A rod of correction imparts wisdom, but a youth left to himself is a disgrace to his mother."* How many children in the United States are left to themselves everyday? Thousands are placed in day-care centers as young as six weeks. Tens of thousands spend more time with paid guardians than they do with their fathers and mothers, if they are blessed to have both. Over six million children between the ages of five and fourteen come home to an empty dwelling each day. These are the latchkey children. The effects of being a latchkey child differ with age. Research has shown that loneliness, boredom, and fear are most common for those ten or younger. In the early teenage years, there is a greater susceptibility to peer pressure, which can result in alcohol abuse, smoking, and sexual experimentation. The effects on their psychological development has shown higher levels of behavioral problems and depression and lower levels of self-esteem than those children who have a mother or some other family member waiting for them when they come home from school. We have a generation of neglected children who will someday be parents. Unless we change our cultural expectations of mothers working outside the home, the cycle will repeat itself with devastating results. The presence of a parent removes the emptiness from an empty house.

Proverbs 29:17: *"Discipline your son, and he will give you comfort; he will also give you delight."* What father could ask for more than for his children to be sources of delight and comfort? The key word here is *discipline*. More than physical correction is implied in Solomon's advice. Every area of your child's life is involved in discipline. Accountability is another way to put it. Whether they are cleaning their rooms, performing assigned chores, completing their homework, practicing their music, playing with the team, or some other task, teach your children the value of responsibility. Many children today have little time to be children. The fault is not theirs. Dads, your child or children do not have to sign up for every sport or school activity. Give them time to grow and enjoy a stage in life that is as fleeting as the dew on the grass. Don't expect your son to fulfill your dream or carry on your legend. God has a special plan for your son or daughter. Your responsibility is to encourage, not force, your children to reach their potential and develop their unique talent.

Crisis

Every family will experience a crisis. Some seem to live in the middle of one. As a friend of mine often says, "You are either headed into a crisis, going through one, or coming out of one." A crisis can blow in from any direction and without warning. The phone may ring. A policeman may knock on your door in the early morning hours. Your pastor may show up unexpectedly with a somber look on his face. The doctor may start his conversation with, "I'm sorry to have to tell you this . . ." Your son's grades may suddenly begin to drop, and he may become withdrawn. Your unmarried daughter may come into your bedroom one night crying to inform you and your wife that you are going to be grandparents. The list goes on and on. Very few have faced a crisis like Job in the Old Testament. In one day, he lost all his earthly possessions and his ten children were killed in a storm. Following those unimaginable events, he lost his health and his wife told him to curse God and die. However, if you will read this insightful book, you will find a man of impeccable character who never lost his faith or his trust in God. Following are some verses Solomon penned for every father faced with a crisis.

Proverbs 10:2: *"Ill gotten gains do not profit anyone, but righteousness rescues from death."* Whether stealing or gambling, if your son becomes involved with the wrong crowd, the money gained from these actions will lead only to poverty, if not financial bankruptcy most certainly spiritual bankruptcy. Teaching your sons and daughters the rewards of righteousness will someday rescue them from disaster.

Proverbs 11:29: *"The one who brings ruin on his household will inherit the wind, and a fool will be a slave to someone whose heart is wise."* Isaac and his wife, Rebekah, are prime examples of parental favoritism. Isaac loved his son Esau more than his younger son Jacob. With Rebekah, it was just the opposite. This prejudice on the part of both parents brought ruin to the house of Isaac. Fathers, showing partiality to one child over another is an invitation to a windstorm that can blow through your family for generations.

Proverbs 17:21: *"A man fathers a fool to his own sorrow; the father of a fool has no joy."* One of the heartbreaks for a godly father is to produce an ungodly child. As I have shared with thousands of fathers across this country and in Great Britain, "All you can do is all you can do, but be sure to do all you can." In the life of every child, a time is reached when they step into adolescence and begin to make their own choices. This is as it should be. If a child has been taught godly principles by a godly father but begins to make choices that are diametrically opposed to those teachings, the result will be a brokenhearted father and mother. Fathers, if you spend your life rescuing your children and answering for their foolish choices, you will eventually destroy your health and most possibly your marriage.

Proverbs 17:25: *"A foolish son is grief to his father and bitterness to the one who bore him."* Many a mother has cried herself to sleep countless times because of a wayward child. She feels her prayers and counsel have been all for nothing. Some children return to the teachings of their fathers and mothers; some children do not. Some children are the gleam in the eyes of their fathers; some children are the tears. Grief and bitterness are heavy burdens to bear and offer only pain when a parent realizes their son or daughter has never returned from Sodom.

Proverbs 18:19: *"An offended brother is harder to reach than a fortified city, and quarrels are like the bars of a fortress."* Living in a family that has experienced severe sibling conflict can create chasms that may never be crossed. As a father, you may have been caught in the crossfire of your children due to a crisis brought on by one or the other. Words spoken in anger, emotions overruling reason, and actions carried out wounds the spirit as well as the body. Just as hate is a choice, so is forgiveness. Teaching your children how to forgive while they are young will help bring healing when future offenses and quarrels erupt. We always taught our children that they were each other's best friend. They were then; they are today.

Proverbs 19:26: *"The one who assaults his father and evicts his mother is a disgraceful and shameful son."* The word *assaults* means to waste. A prime example is the man Judas Iscariot, one of Jesus' disciples. What a waste his life was. He undoubtedly behaved as a boy in the manner he did as a man. From what he did to Jesus, you can reasonably deduct he did to his own parents. If he would deceitfully steal from the purse of the disciples, he would do the same to his parents. A man who would betray the Son of God would give no thought to wasting his father's possessions and leaving his mother in the streets to beg. This type of son goes beyond prodigal to pure evil. The crisis he creates is only laid to rest when he is. The consequences of his choices, however, continue to live beyond the grave. Judas will forever be known as the betrayer. His family name *Iscariot* is eternally linked to a son who wasted his life.

Final Thoughts

As a father, my prayer for you is that your children will bring joy to your life and comfort to your soul. Nothing is so beautiful on earth than a home where Jesus is the unseen yet always present member of the family. Introduce him to your children while they are young. Teach them his truths. Instruct them in his ways. Above all, unlike Solomon, what you instill into their hearts live before them in your life. The greatest title a father can ever possess is DADDY. The greatest joy for a father is to hear the word *daddy* spoken out of love and respect. May it be so with you and your children. Remember, *"Unless the LORD builds the house, they labor in vain who build it"* (Psalm 127:1).

I would appreciate any comments or questions you might have now that you have finished reading the book. This text was written to encourage all fathers from the heart of a father. God's blessings on you and your family.

DR. JERRY DRACE
hopeforthehome@juno.com